Santa's Smelly Socks!

Words & Pictures by:
Len Foley

Published by:
MONTY THE DOG PRODUCTIONS

For Soapy Sails

Words © 2020 Len Foley
Pictures © 2020 Len Foley
Cover and internal design © 2020 Len Foley

All rights reserved. No part of this book may be reproduced or transmitted in any form or by any means whatsoever without express written permission from the author, except in the case of brief quotations embodied in critical articles and reviews. Please refer all pertinent questions to the publisher.

Thanks to my genius editor (and wife) for all her incredible insights: Rebecca Gauthier. And special thanks to: Lilia Saleba, Eden Ray, Evangeline Ray, Jack Cummings, Kara Henderson, & Sofia Foley! Additional thanks to: Laurel Bylin, Riley Glasgow, Christina Warfield, Azelina Fontenot, Titus Ray, Malachi Ray, River Gauthier and James Michael Cummings.

A long time ago,
On a cold, snowy night

Santa flew his magic sleigh
When he beheld a strange sight.

A GIANT stack-of-socks
Piled HIGH upon the road

A few miles FURTHER
Another stinky load!

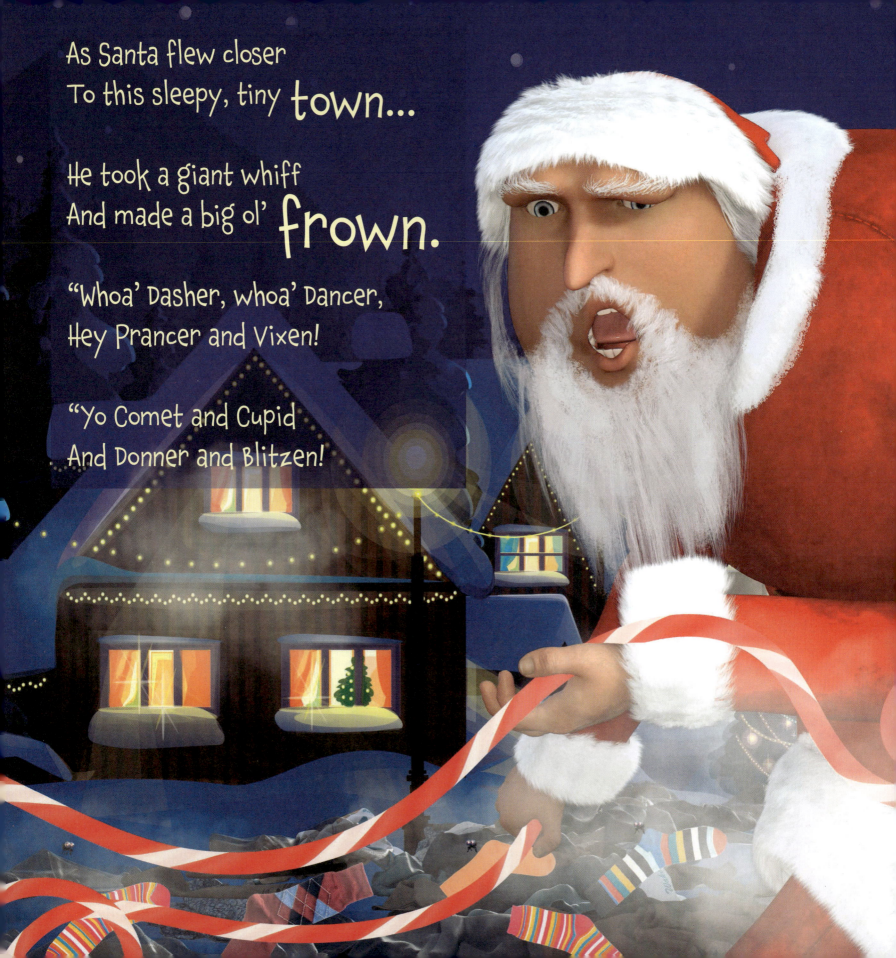

As Santa flew closer
To this sleepy, tiny town...

He took a giant whiff
And made a big ol' frown.

"Whoa' Dasher, whoa' Dancer,
Hey Prancer and Vixen!

"Yo Comet and Cupid
And Donner and Blitzen!

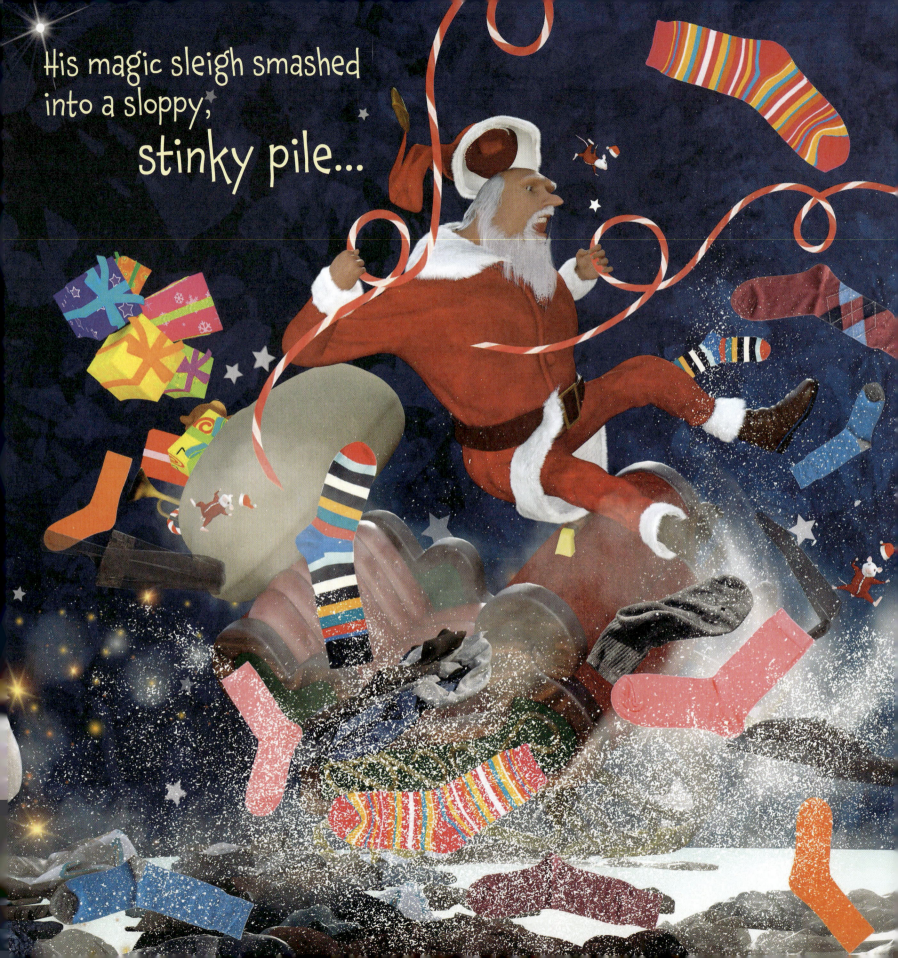
His magic sleigh smashed into a sloppy, stinky pile...

Kris Kringle pulled out 'Elf Suds' soap and dropped down to his **knees.**

He washed the steamy, smelly mess in a cold and snowy **stream.**

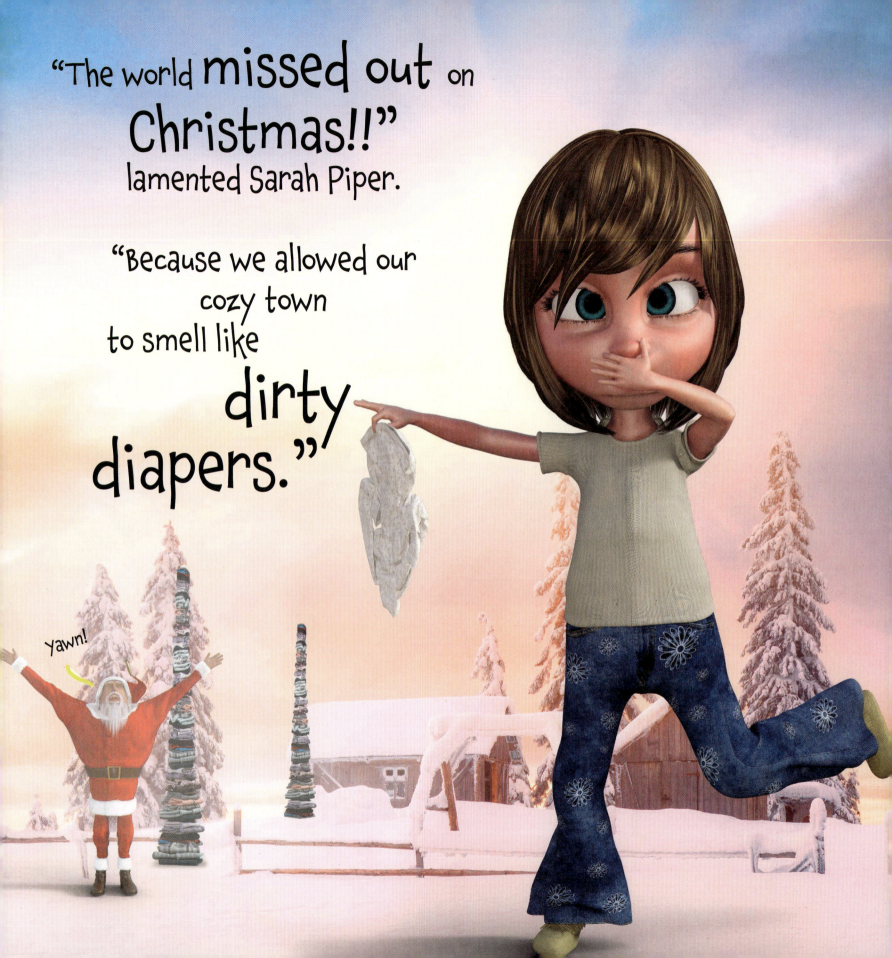

That's when little Lucas who **never** washed at all,

tugged on Santa's arm Who stood so proud and tall.

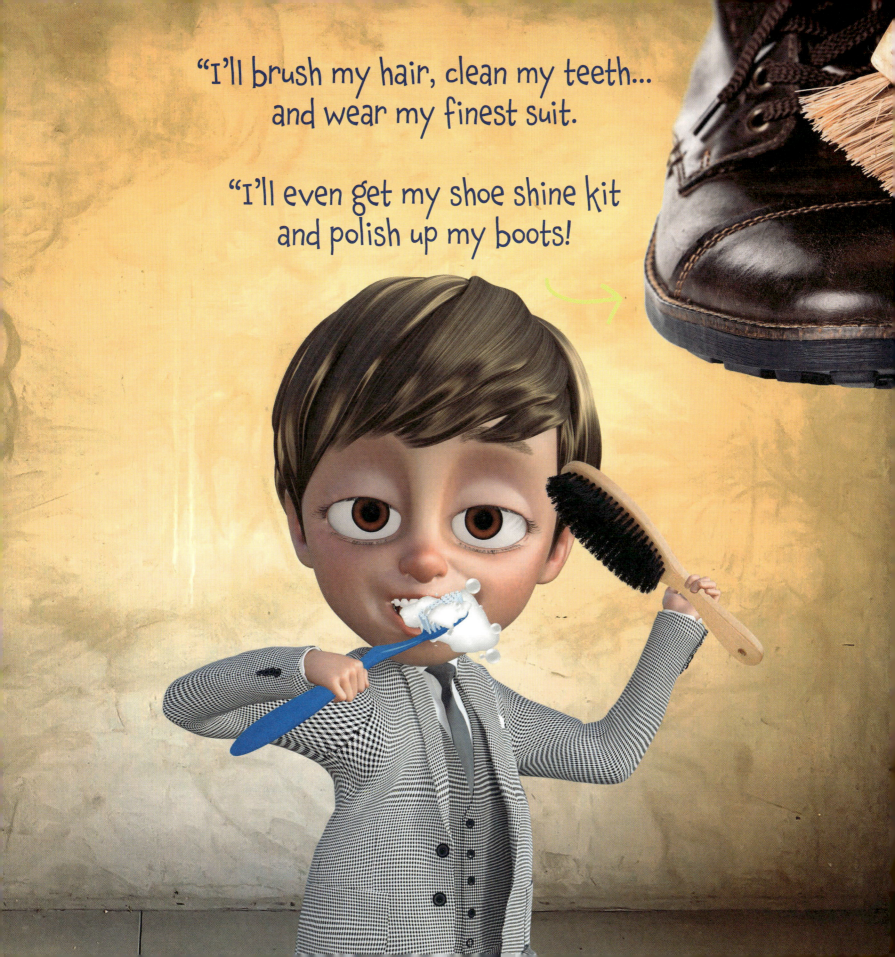

"I'll brush my hair, clean my teeth... and wear my finest suit.

"I'll even get my shoe shine kit and polish up my boots!

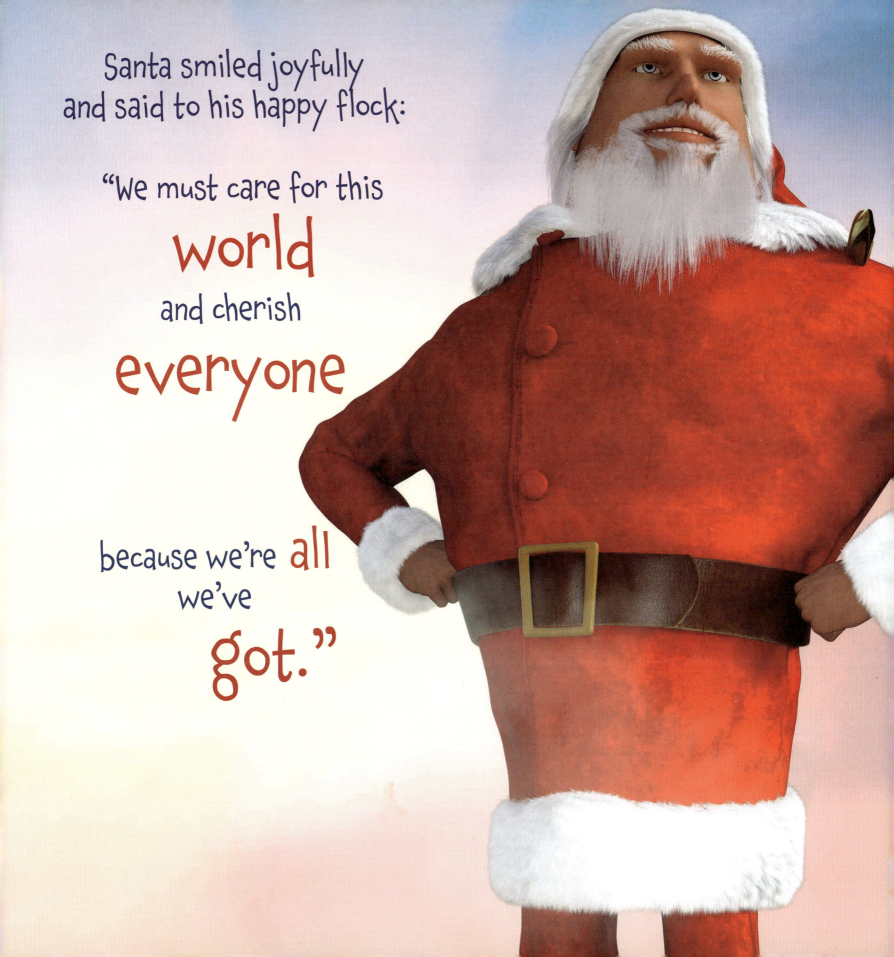

Santa smiled joyfully and said to his happy flock:

"We must care for this **world** and cherish **everyone** because we're **all** we've **got.**"

"And if you promise to care for your own precious spot

"I will leave some gifts inside each of your socks."

MORE HILARIOUS BOOKS FROM LEN FOLEY!

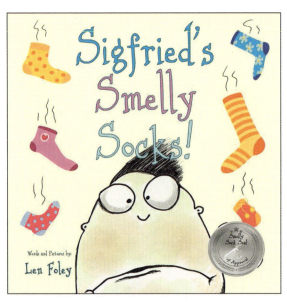
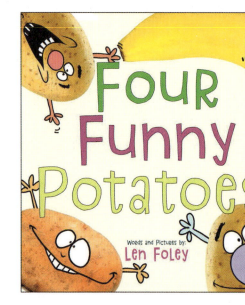
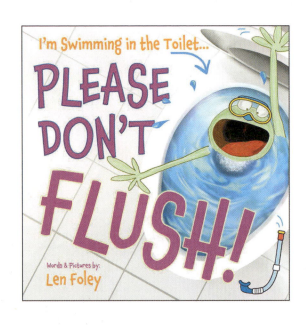
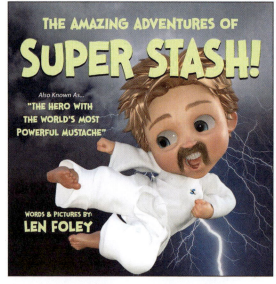

Available January 2021

For more info, visit: www.LenFoley.com